Compliance
and
Governance

Know What You Need to Know

Compliance and Governance

Know What You Need to Know

Dr. Amy Jauman

National Institute for Social Media

ISBN: 978-1-946649-06-5

Special thanks to the following content reviewers from the National Institute for Social Media community. We appreciate your feedback and continued support!

- Jennifer Radke, SMS
- Kimberly Behzadi, MBA, SMS
- Taylor Lizura
- Toni Pirtle, SMS

What is the National Institute for Social Media (NISM)?

The National Institute for Social Media (NISM) is an organization dedicated to social media certification and education for professional social media practitioners. In partnership with organizations and lifelong learning enthusiasts, they've created a community for professional development and set the standards for social media education, assessment and certification, and consulting. NISM provides the foremost Social Media Strategy (SMS) certification exam in the US, which allows social media professionals to obtain a recognized professional standard in this continually developing field.

Why does NISM provide a certification for social media professionals?

A certification in any industry is an unbiased, standard measurement of an individual's ability to perform specific skills. NISM realized the need for a certification within the realm of social media as more and more individuals entered the field with varying levels of experience. How could experienced social media professionals demonstrate their knowledge? How could hiring managers identify individuals with the skill set in social media strategy they desired? A professional certification is the perfect solution. The SMS certification covers six content domains (Strategic Planning, Community Management, Marketing and Communications, Compliance and Governance,

Project Management, and Research and Analysis) that ensure each person who successfully passes the exam has the depth and breadth needed to be considered a professional social media strategist. In addition to passing this rigorous exam, individuals must continue to update and enhance their skills in order to stay current with their certification, through continuing education courses, workshops, and conferences. The National Institute for Social Media also requires all NISM-certified Social Media Strategists (SMS) to adhere to a strict code of ethics.

NISM has built its community of social media professionals around five core values:

Trust – for both the confidence in the works we do for our customers and the value we add to the industry as a whole, through hard work, honesty and integrity.

Community – it is our belief that in order to create a positive community we need to not only find ways to use our skills to support each other, but to also encourage others around us to participate and get involved as well.

Respect – as a fundamental building block for all relationships, it is imperative that we treat others as we want to be treated and to acknowledge and promote the great work of our colleagues and peers.

Quality – at our core we recognize that the value we provide to our community hinges on quality. Our dedication to standards and external industry credentialing is key to our success.

Lifelong Learning – with the rate at which social media changes, we realize that if we are not in constant learning mode we will fall behind and fail to stay relevant. We promote lifelong learning within our community and as an industry at large.

Who's the author?

Dr. Amy Jauman is a certified Social Media Strategist and lead instructor at the National Institute for Social Media. She is a social media consultant, writer and professor and her formal education includes a master's degree in experiential education, so you'll find plenty of real-world application prompts. She also has a doctorate in organization development, so there's a lot of information about how to work with people in a variety of business environments. Her interest in helping people prepare for and pass the SMS certification exam was piqued in 2011 when she began looking for ways she could establish her credibility in social media.

Dr. Jauman discovered that many of her peers working in social media and students venturing out as marketing professionals had the same need for social media credentials that accurately represented their knowledge and experience. When presented with the chance to write these books and provide students and professionals with a practical guide to the six content domains covered in the SMS certification exam, she jumped at the opportunity.

Who should read this book?

There are likely three groups of people who would benefit most from reading this book, although it is of value to anyone with an interest in social media compliance and governance.

Anyone prepping to take the SMS certification exam. If you're thinking about taking the SMS exam, you've probably discovered that compliance and governance is one of six content domains covered in the exam. Whether or not you're familiar with the concept of compliance and governance, this book can be a great way to quickly and easily check out what's covered on the exam. It can also help you identify areas you might want to learn more about before your exam.

Anyone considering a role that is entirely or in part associated with compliance and governance. It's possible that the depth and breadth of the SMS certification exam doesn't interest you. If you're more interested in one area of social media – working exclusively in compliance and governance as opposed to the broader role of being a certified social media strategist – this book can provide you with insights specific to your area of interest. One of the reasons we transitioned from a single, large textbook to six smaller books was to connect with the social media professionals interested in joining our community through their expertise in one or two of the content domains.

Anyone considering hiring a compliance and governance expert. It's possible that you aren't even interested in social media strategy or certification – but you're smart enough to know it's important. This book can act as a great guide for any leader in any industry considering adding a social media compliance and governance expert to the team.

However you're connected to the National Institute for Social Media (NISM) and whatever you'd like to learn from this book, we invite you to connect with us. Find us on Facebook at facebook.com/NISMPulse, Twitter @NISMPulse or any of the sites listed at nismonline.org.

The National Institute for Social Media Code of Ethics

The Code of Ethics is intended to reflect the standards and behavior that National Institute for Social Media ("NISM") certified practitioners and program applicants expect of each other as they perform their duties and that reaffirm the value of holding an NISM credential. The purpose of the Code of Ethics is to ensure public confidence in the integrity and service of NISM-certified professionals while performing their duties.

The Code of Ethics identifies the types of circumstances that may compromise the reliability of NISM's ability to establish, or certify, a certificate holder's or program applicant's ability to perform the essential tasks of the vocation with at least minimal competency. For purposes of this Code of Ethics, "essential tasks" are defined as the general vocational duties that are expected to be performed by NISM-certified professionals. "Minimal competency" is defined as the ability to perform the essential tasks effectively, with minimal supervision.

NISM does not monitor on-the-job behavior or actions. Adherence to these ethical standards is expected from all certificate holders and applicants. Any violation may be subject to removal of his or her certified status.

All NISM certificate holders and applicants are expected to adhere to the following standards of professional conduct and ethics:

1. We represent ourselves truthfully, honestly, and to the best of our abilities throughout the entire certification process, and in performance of the essential tasks described in section 3 of the candidate handbook.

2. We adhere to all exam site rules, making no attempt to complete an exam dishonestly or to assist any other person in doing so.
3. We protect proprietary or confidential information that has been entrusted to us as if it were our own.
4. We state only what we know to be true, and are clear about opinions and assumptions vs. facts.
5. We are transparent about who we are, and whom or what we represent online.
6. We take ownership of our online activities, the content we have created, and any missteps we have made along the way.
7. We uphold the policies, rules, regulations and laws that govern our activities.
8. We report unethical or illegal conduct to appropriate authorities.

Contents

Introduction

Compliance and Governance

What do social media strategists need to know about compliance and governance? To what degree are we responsible for the seemingly innumerable laws that could be associated with social media? Are some laws more relevant – or interpreted differently – in some areas of social media? With so many laws to keep track of, how can we possibly keep up?

Those are all great questions, and most social media strategists have struggled with them at one point or another in their career. There is naturally some fear associated with the responsibility of managing a digital presence, but most professionals quickly realize the key is to stay up-to-date and informed enough to know what you need and when you should ask for help. This book is written in that spirit.

> The following information is intended to guide people interested in learning more about the legal considerations associated with a legal and ethical social media strategy.
> It is not intended to be advice.
> If you have questions about a specific situation related to your social media presence, consult a legal professional.

It can be overwhelming to think about what you need to know related to social media law. This book is designed to help social media professionals understand some of the legal terminology associated with managing a professional social media presence. In fact, the glossary of this book is twice the size of the other NISM books! We'll also share examples and instructions that can help you better understand how these practices can be implemented in your environment. And most importantly, learning more about compliance and governance can help you identify areas in which you need to request help from a legal professional.

If you're preparing to take the certified SMS exam through the National Institute for Social Media, there are a few key concepts outlined in this book you'll want to pay attention to:

Compliance
Obedience or conformity, typically in reference to an established law or policy.

- How to create a social media policy to govern activities
- Maintaining a social media policy as change occurs
- Monitoring "Terms of Service" to protect your company's intellectual property interests
- Defining when and when not to participate in a conversation
- Creating a procedure explaining how to participate and converse in a variety of situations
- Working with key stakeholders to ensure efforts are supported

Governance
Directing a group through structured, sustained, and regulated processes to abide by laws and norms.

As you can see, the key areas of the exam are focused on how you as a social media professional can support your team as you all participate in executing the organization's social media strategy. But we wanted to provide you with more information than that – we wanted to give you the opportunity to consider the many different legal considerations you might face.

NISM 2016 Social Media Job Study

54.5% of participants ranked planning and goal setting as a task of high importance. This is an increase of 34.3% from the 2012 study.

25.9% of those surveyed spend more than 10 hours each week on project management tasks.

Each content domain increased in importance from 2012 to 2016.

The most important task within Marketing & Communications was

Branding

66.5% identified it as highly important.

The NISM 2016 Social Media Job Study

43 states.
20 industries.
533 men and women.
Managers, employees and consultants.

68.8% of participants cited acting appropriately without direction as highly important. It was perceived as important in 2012 as well, but only 43.6% chose **highly important.**

Responding to comments increased from low to high importance between 2012 and 2016.

#NISM2016JS

Content domains explored through the job study are the same as the SMS exam.

Project Management
Governance & Compliance
Marketing & Communications
Research & Analysis
Strategic Planning
Community

The value of 2-way communication with customers increased from medium to high importance.

www.nismonline.org

Part One
Intellectual Property

Chapter 1

NISM Job Study Results

In the 2016 NISM Social Media Job Study, designed to understand the key responsibilities of social media strategists, we asked about the prevalence and importance of compliance and governance. Compliance and governance was described to survey participants as:

> *"...the development of policies and establishment of legal limitations for a social media team. Growth can quickly be stifled by legal obstacles, particularly when businesses use external social platforms, so careful management of this aspect of a social media account is critical."*

The survey questions focused on the following four aspects of compliance and governance:

- Monitoring "Terms of Service" to protect a company's intellectual property interests
- Creating and maintaining social media policy
- Creating a procedure explaining how to participate and converse in a variety of situations
- Acting appropriately without direction (self-starter)

In the first social media job study conducted by NISM in 2012, compliance and governance was generally given a low importance ranking. By 2016, each category appears to have gained importance in the eyes of social media professionals – the largest percentage in each category ranked the task as highly important. A few of the highlights from the survey include:

- In 2012, 11.4% of the participants surveyed ranked the creation of a social media policy as highly important. In 2016 that percentage increased to 36.1%.
- Though the value of these tasks appears to have increased, time spent on each task has not. This could simply be because much of the work is identified and then passed on to an expert, or it could be an indication that social media professionals realize something is important but don't commit time to it.
- The need to be able to work independently and without direction was a popular topic on our online survey and in our follow-up interviews. In 2012, 43.6% of the respondents ranked it as highly important – the most common selection. And in 2016 it was still the most common selection, but 68.8% of the respondents ranked it as highly important. Is this because leaders across all industries are realizing just how important it is to have a social media professional they can rely on to keep up with trends?

Survey participants were given the opportunity to share additional thoughts about the importance of compliance and governance. Here are a few of the quotes we found most interesting.

- In a big organization, let's face it, what's put on social media will be reviewed by many people, including legal, so autonomy isn't a facet of the job.
- In my capacity as an educator and trainer, I am unaware of the time spent by the social media professionals who manage the areas of compliance and governance at my institution or specific client organizations.
- We work very closely with our legal team to review any policies we have in place.

Remember, this book is for educational purposes only. If you have specific questions, you should always ask a legal professional.

We did things like make friends with the lawyers first because I think every social media manager would probably say, "OK, one of the struggles you have is with legal, because they're going to tell you, 'No, you can't do anything.'"

And you're going to say, "Well, the rest of the world is doing this on social media, and consumers are forcing us to do this, so we're going to have to do it eventually."

So we just slowly get closer and closer to the middle where we both compromise and can do something.

> \- Social Media Manager
> NISM 2016 Job Study

Chapter 1 Discussion

1. Download the most recent copy of the Social Media Job Study from nismonline.org. Read the results from the compliance and governance section and identify at least three survey results that were meaningful to you – either because they surprised you or because you can use the information in conversations with your team or clients.

2. Share the Social Media Job Study with your legal advisor (familiar with social media and marketing or not) and ask for their thoughts on each of the areas measured and what areas they think your organization should focus on.

Chapter 2

Intellectual Property?

I ntellectual property is work that is the result of creativity to which one has rights and for which one may apply for a patent, copyright, or trademark. There are two primary reasons you need to comprehend intellectual property:

1. It's important for you to understand what your intellectual property is so you can protect it.
2. It's equally important for you to understand which intellectual property belongs to others so you can use it correctly (which might mean not at all).

This second point is especially important for social media strategists to understand because the sharing of content is easy and often encouraged on social media platforms. As a result of all of the possible ways content can move around social media, keeping track of your content and following the rules associated with content that belongs to others can be difficult.

> **Intellectual Property**
>
> Work that is the result of creativity to which one has rights and for which one may apply for a patent, copyright, or trademark.

Terms of Service

Creating and sharing terms of service can be a great start to educating your internal team and your customers about intellectual property. As a social media professional, the terms of service (sometimes called terms of use) you create for your organization are essentially a list of rules and guidelines that a user must agree to in order to use your product. Going through the process of writing terms of service or reading the existing terms you have might also help you understand what you can and can't do with various content.

- Creating Terms of Service (or Terms of Use) helps people understand how they are allowed to use your content.
- Reading Terms of Service will help you and your team avoid incorrect usage and potentially expensive violations of intellectual property use.

Text is available under the Creative Commons Attribution-ShareAlike License; additional terms may apply. By using this site, you agree to the Terms of Use and Privacy Policy. Wikipedia® is a registered trademark of the Wikimedia Foundation, Inc., a non-profit organization.

Wikipedia has an excellent approach to introducing their terms of use. At the bottom of the site, they have this disclaimer:

As you can see, by using the website, you automatically agree to the Terms of Use and Privacy Policy. So, what exactly did you agree to?

Terms of Use

This is a human-readable **summary** of the Terms of Use

Disclaimer: This summary is not a part of the Terms of Use and is not a legal document. It is simply a handy reference for understanding the full terms. Think of it as the user-friendly interface to the legal language of our Terms of Use.

Part of our mission is to:

- **Empower and Engage** people around the world to collect and develop educational content and either publish it under a free license or dedicate it to the public domain.
- **Disseminate** this content effectively and globally, free of charge.

You are free to:

- **Read and Print** our articles and other media free of charge.
- **Share and Reuse** our articles and other media under free and open licenses.
- **Contribute To and Edit** our various sites or Projects.

Under the following conditions:

- **Responsibility** – You take responsibility for your edits (since we only *host* your content).
- **Civility** – You support a civil environment and do not harass other users.
- **Lawful Behavior** – You do not violate copyright or other laws.
- **No Harm** – You do not harm our technology infrastructure.
- **Terms of Use and Policies** – You adhere to the below Terms of Use and to the applicable community policies when you visit our sites or participate in our communities.

With the understanding that:

- **You License Freely Your Contributions** – you generally must license your contributions and edits to our sites or Projects under a free and open license (unless your contribution is in the public domain).
- **No Professional Advice** – the content of articles and other projects is for informational purposes only and does not constitute professional advice.

First, Wikipedia provides a summary of their terms of use – identifying the summary as "human-readable." It's clear they want more than legal coverage from their terms; they want people to understand how the site is meant to be used.

Further down the page, further details are explored including their privacy policy, trademarks, and a long list of other considerations. I believe Wikipedia would deem those details as not "human readable," but, like all organizations, they recognize the importance of the information.

Reading Terms of Service

Lifehacker tackled this very topic in 2012, sharing the following statistics:

"A recent paper from Carnegie Mellon suggests it would take the average Internet user about 76 days to read all their privacy policies. The researchers found that of the top 75 websites, the average length of a privacy policy is 2,514 words. Of course, for every privacy policy a Terms of Service, end

user agreement, or other contract also exists. So, how can we feasibly parse all this information without spending 8 hours a day on it?"

How can a social media professional review terms of service efficiently?

- Consider the content you're reviewing. Are there any elements you need to be aware of for the purposes of your work? (E.g., if you were reading the terms of service associated with a photo-sharing website, you might pay special attention to the sharing limitations.)
- Review the bold headings to identify the information that's important to you. That will allow you to focus your attention where it needs to be.
- When in doubt, get a second opinion! A big part of being a successful social media strategist is being able to identify when you need to get more information.

A lot of people have never read terms of service, much less revised or written them. But as a social media professional, it is your responsibility to know how to navigate their details efficiently.

Infringement
Use without permission of an invention for which someone else owns a patent, copyright or trademark, whether the violation was intentional or not.

Writing Terms of Service

If you are creating your own terms of service from scratch, talk to your legal advisor about the best way to proceed. If they recommend that you create terms of service for them to review, there are many templates available online that can help you get started. Before adding the details, talk to your advisor and agree on a template that's a good starting point for your business. If you're creating something from scratch or working on an existing document, check to see if these terms are represented.

Privacy Policy

How an organization gathers, manages, and discloses some or all of its customer and client information.

License

Permission from an approved figure to own or use something, or perform a trade.

Trademark

Symbol, word, or words legally registered or established by use as representing a company or product.

Chapter 2 Discussion

1. Review three separate terms of service written for organizations you're familiar with. Compare and contrast them, paying special attention to any of the differences that might relate to your business specifically.

2. Consider how you would explain intellectual property to your team. Create a document, infographic, or presentation that would help you explain to them the importance of protecting your intellectual property and not misusing intellectual property.

Chapter 3

Terms You Need to Know

We mentioned at the very beginning of this book that our focus is to educate you – to help you understand the language associated with social media law and to help you identify when you should ask for additional help. In this chapter, we're going to introduce you to some of the most common terms you'll hear when talking about social media and marketing laws and briefly describe why you might need to understand the words in each category. Since many social media laws are only just now being created or are being updated on a regular basis, it's important to do more than just read this book once and familiarize yourself with the terms that follow. We encourage you to set up push/pull habits so you can keep yourself informed:

- Set up "push notifications" from trusted websites that provide social media newsletters or a general alert (like a Google alert for specific terms) to ensure that you are frequently reminded to review changes in the industry.
- Make it part of another routine – weekly meetings, your Monday morning check-in, etc. – to "pull" articles, updates, etc. related to changes in social media.

The following information will provide you with a great base for understanding social media compliance and governance. But to avoid breaking the evolving laws and guidelines created by various governing agencies, it's critical that you commit to practices that will ensure you regularly receive updates.

Protecting Your Intellectual Property

The first set of terms all refer to different ways individuals and organizations may protect their intellectual property. If you work in social media, it's important to have a basic understanding of what each of these terms means and how they might apply to the work you do. For example, you may have just read about consumer privacy and wondered what your organization's consumer privacy policy is. Reviewing it on your own, with your team, or with your legal advisor is a great way to solidify your understanding of the term and how it might affect your environment. Your additional questions might even help others around you learn a little more about their organization.

Trademark

A *trademark* is a symbol, word, or words legally registered or established by use as representing a company or product. You might also hear people refer to a *registered* trademark, which refers to a word or symbol registered with a national trademark office.

Patent

A *patent* is a government license awarding a right for a set period that prohibits others from making, selling, or using the item described. In social media, patents are often sought for apps, processes, and tools.

Copyright

Copyright refers to the legal right of ownership granted to the creator of any artistic work. When someone creates something, it is automatically covered by copyright law. In social media, this commonly refers to photography, art, video, and written work, but can cover any creative piece. Like trademarks, you can also have a *registered copyright*, meaning the date and content of a protected work was recorded through a verifiable government source.

Confidentiality

Confidentiality refers to anything private that can't be disclosed to a wider group. This is less tangible than the previous three terms and more of a concept associated with many different kinds of law – including social media.

Consumer Privacy

Like confidentiality, *consumer privacy* is a concept or idea that directly affects most businesses. It refers to the laws and regulations designed to protect individuals from loss of privacy due to failures of corporate customer privacy measures. If an organization doesn't understand consumer privacy, it is at risk of making very costly mistakes.

Publicity Rights

Publicity rights refer to the control of the commercial use of a name, image, likeness, or other aspects of an identity. Whether you are the owner of the rights or the person at risk of infringing on those rights, it's important to have a clear agreement of how the identity in question can be used.

Are you wondering what you might be protecting? In addition to any kind of intellectual property as discussed in the previous chapter, you and other creatives and business owners are protecting anything you might want to keep private to ensure your business is successful. This information can be anything – a formula, a concept or process, the prototype for a new invention. The idea is that it sets your business apart in the market and, therefore, you need to work to protect it.

Proprietary Information

Proprietary information includes any processes, items and methods used in business which an organization wishes to keep private. Proprietary information is often associated with a competitive edge. Proprietary information is also called *trade secrets*.

Breaking and Bending the Law (Policies or Guidelines)

The next set of terms all talk about how you or others might break or bend social media law. Does it feel like a fine line? Are you wondering how you should define fair use and if something you created really counts as a parody? If you're asking yourself those questions, you're off to a great start. The question now is, what should you do next? A few good options include:

- Bring your specific questions to your legal advisor. It's a great learning opportunity, but seeking a professional opinion is also the most responsible approach any social media professional can take when faced with a legal question.
- Do some research on your own. If you've uncovered a concept or a term you'd like to learn more about, iden-tify a credible resource (e.g., the Federal Trade Com-mission website or a publication recommended by your legal advisor) and do your own research. Looking for examples and reading various interpretations is a great way to learn and remember new information – as long as you continue to consult with an expert before mak-ing any decisions.

Copyright Violation

A *copyright violation* is any misuse of a protected artistic work. It's important to remember that, in the United States, creators aren't required to use the copyright symbol to protect their work. Never assume work is available for you to use.

Fair Use

There are times you can use protected work legally. *Fair use is the principle that supports the use of brief excerpts of copyright material under certain circumstances.* Material can be quoted verbatim under fair use for criticism, news reporting, teaching, and research, without permission from or payment to the copyright holder. It's important to consider how you would defend using the materials and to get a second opinion from a legal professional before using any protected work. Similarly, there are also *safe harbor laws* which deem certain conduct not to violate a specific rule, typically as the result of a connection with a separate and less specific rule.

Parody

Another way you can use protected work is a *parody*. Parody refers to an exaggerated comedic imitation of the style of a particular individual or group. It is protected as free speech as long as it's deemed that the average person understands it is satirical in nature.

An example of a parody – or rather, a string of parodies – would be when GEICO (an insurance company) created a commercial where their mascot (a gecko) reviews and provides feedback on his own commercials, throws a wild party, or sails a boat. The average person would never believe a gecko was really doing any of these things that a spokesperson would do.

Contributing to Your Community

In a later chapter, you'll learn about Creative Commons – a nonprofit organization that gathers cultural, educational, and scientific content in "the commons" that's made available to the public for free and legal sharing, use, repurposing, and remixing. The following terms are associated with Creative Commons licensing, but you might see them used in other scenarios as well, so we wanted to introduce them in this chapter.

Attribution

Attribution refers to identifying a person as the creator of a specific work.

License
Permission from an approved figure to own or use something, or perform a trade.

Share Alike Use

Share alike use is a copyright licensing term that requires copies or adaptations of a work be released under the same or similar license as the original.

Commercial and Non-commercial Use

When the term *commercial use* is used, it refers to any act or process that generates a profit. *Non-commercial use* refers to actions not primarily intended for compensation.

Derivative Work

A derivative work is anything created from or based on existing work.

Terms You Need to Know
(Related to Tactics You Should Avoid)

There are also terms you need to know for actions that are universally considered unethical – and many of them are now closely monitored and penalized in various ways. Why is it important for you to know these terms?

You might hear someone describing one of these processes and be tempted to try it for a "quick win" without thinking through the potential consequences.

Your team, client, or key stakeholders may inquire about some of these practices. It's important that you can speak about them in a clear and concise manner and provide advice accordingly.

Just because you aren't doing it doesn't mean other people will make the same choices. Unfortunately, you need to be aware of the potential unethical practices your competitors may be using so you can protect yourself accordingly.

Black Hat Marketing

In a digital marketing campaign, *black hat marketing* refers to techniques or practices that are illegal or unethical. They are usually completed by practitioners looking to get fast results, but those results rarely last as black hat practices are usually uncovered and the results reversed by search engines and platform owners. The opposite approach is called white hat marketing.

Defamation

Defamation refers to the act of damaging a person's reputation with untrue or misrepresented information – intentionally or not. By the end of 2016, it was easiest to find examples of potential defamation cases in the surge of fake news that became so popular during the most recent U.S. election. Individuals and brands had the potential to be targets of defamation – or the perpetrators.

Brandjacking

It's hard to deny intent with *brandjacking*! This refers to the practice of securing the online identity of another individual or business for the purposes of acquiring that person's or business's brand equity.

Cybersquatting

Cybersquatting is the practice of registering internet domain names in the hope of reselling them at a profit. This does require some skill and risk, as the cybersquatter has to be the first to realize what domain names will become valuable.

Lampooning

Lampooning refers to satire or ridicule directed at an individual, institution, or item, focused on the character or behavior of the same.

A Few More Important Terms...

We'll end this chapter with a set of random terms you might encounter as you spend more time working on social media law. Some of these might be familiar to you – perhaps even from work outside of social media.

Dilution

In marketing, *dilution* refers to the decreased value related to excessive use and/or increased availability of a product. This is a delicate balance in many markets – and may be out of your brand's control. For example, if your competitors suddenly double within a year, there may simply be too many options in your market for the number of consumers.

White Hat

In a digital marketing campaign, this refers to techniques or practices that are legal and ethical. These are the best practices for long-term, sustainable success. The opposite approach is called black hat marketing.

Brand Equity

You *brand equity* is the commercial value associated with a product. It is based solely on consumer perception as opposed to the product or service itself.

Contract

A *contract* is a written or spoken agreement between two or more parties meant to be enforceable by law.

Waiver

A *waiver* is a statement giving up a right. You have most likely heard of this associated with a person signing a waiver acknowledging risk involved in an activity.

Cookies

Though you might think of a tasty after-school snack, in social media, cookies actually refer to messages from web servers shared to your browser when you visit internet sites. Depending on how they're set up, cookies can tell a website owner the kind of device a person is working on, the software you're using, or other personal information. Cookies are described in website privacy policies and will vary greatly by organization.

Commercial Speech

Commercial speech is language used on behalf of an organization or individual to generate a profit.

As you continue to read this text – and the other NISM textbooks – and visit external sites to learn more information, I encourage you to record any additional terms that are new or even unfamiliar. It's important to start with a solid understanding of social media language before moving on to interpret and apply larger concepts. It's important to remember, too, social media strategists certified through the National Institute for Social Media are bound by the NISM Code of Ethics. Understanding the terminology is the first step to following guidelines, policies and laws. And that understanding is what will keep you from an ethical violation that could put your certification status at risk.

Chapter 3 Discussion

1. Identify three terms that were new to you or that you learned more about in this chapter. Create a graphic or presentation to describe each term and share it with someone else. Answer any questions they might have and use their questions to improve your understanding.

2. Reflect on each of the sections in this chapter. What terms or practices aren't happening in your organization that should be? What did you identify that is happening that should be stopped?

Chapter 4

Creative Commons

"Creative Commons helps you legally share your knowledge and creativity to build a more equitable, accessible, and innovative world. We unlock the full potential of the internet to drive a new era of development, growth and productivity. With a network of staff, board, and affiliates around the world, Creative Commons provides free, easy-to-use copyright licenses to make a simple and standardized way to give the public permission to share and use your creative work–on conditions of your choice."

- creativecommons.org

As we learned earlier in this book, when someone creates something – an image, written work, photograph, etc. – it is automatically covered by copyright law – which is great! But sometimes we want people to use our creative works and we want to use the creative work of other people. Creative Commons allows us all to share our creative works to the extent we want to.

Terms You Need to Know

There are five symbols and seven license types you'll see on Creative Commons. The four symbols are combined in a variety of ways to help creators clearly define how they will allow their works to be used.

Symbol	Name	Description
![Attribution icon]	Attribution	You must acknowledge the author of this work if you use it, and comply with any conditions they require (such as, for example, a link back to their website)
![No Derivative Works icon]	No Derivative Works	You can only use this work as it is. You are not allowed to adapt or modify it.
![Share Alike icon]	Share Alike	If you create anything that is based on this work, you must share it with other people under the same license as the original work.
![Non-commercial icon]	Non-commercial	You must not use this work, or anything based on this work, for commercial purposes.
![Copyright icon]	Copyright	The creator has exclusive rights to the work. You must not use this work.

The seven regularly used licenses are:

Creative Commons

CC0

Freeing content globally without restrictions

BY

Attribution alone

BY-SA

Attribution + ShareAlike

BY-NC

Attribution + Noncommercial

BY-ND

Attribution + NoDerivatives

BY-NC-SA

Attribution + Noncommercial + ShareAlike

BY-NC-ND

Attribution + Noncommercial + NoDerivatives

Why is Creative Commons so important to social media professionals?

If you study compliance and governance long enough, you may start to feel like you can't safely share anything. That idea is the opposite of the goal of most social media strategies. Creative Commons – in addition to really understanding the laws that govern intellectual property – can help you and your team easily access and understand the rules that govern creative work and share that work as each creator intended.

Businesses of any kind should appreciate Creative Commons – and especially your understanding of Creative Commons – as it allows them to collaborate safely and affordably with artists around the world. It's more than just a safe legal move; it's the perfect place for people with diverse backgrounds to come together and share their talents.

Chapter 4 Discussion

1. Visit the Creative Commons website and view the short videos they have that explain the process. Note any new information you find or additional questions you might have. Discuss what you learned with a friend or professional peer.

2. Not everyone has always supported Creative Commons. Like most ideas, there are people who think sharing information this way can be harmful or that the process should be modified somehow. Search the internet for people expressing concern about Creative Commons and consider their viewpoint. Do you agree or disagree with them?

Part Two
Engagement with the Public

Chapter 5

The Federal Trade Commission

As we've said earlier in the book – and will continue to say about any legal considerations associated with your social media presence – any specific questions or concerns should be addressed by a legal professional. However, there are many resources, groups, and organizations that can help social media professionals educate themselves about current social media regulations. One of these organizations is the Federal Trade Commission (FTC).

Initial thoughts related to the FTC might be ones of fear or anxiety. After all, no one wants to be investigated by the FTC – even if they haven't done anything wrong. But it's important for social media professionals to shift their thinking and realize that:

1. The FTC protects consumers – which is always a good thing. If you're an ethical organization following white hat marketing practices, you shouldn't have anything to worry about. If you do make an honest mistake and the FTC identifies the violation and investigates your organization, whatever the penalties, it's important to recognize they aren't targeting you; they are protecting all consumers.

2. The FTC provides excellent materials that are typically easy for the average person to read and understand. If you view them as a regulatory agency you try to avoid, you're forfeiting access to great materials that can help you, your organization, and your consumers.

According to their website in December 2016, the FTC's mission is:

"To prevent business practices that are anticompetitive or deceptive or unfair to consumers; to enhance informed consumer choice and public understanding of the competitive process; and to accomplish this without unduly burdening legitimate business activity."

And their strategic goals are to:

1. Protect Consumers: Prevent fraud, deception, and unfair business practices in the marketplace.
2. Maintain Competition: Prevent anticompetitive mergers and other anticompetitive business practices in the marketplace.
3. Advance Performance: Advance the FTC's performance through organizational, individual, and management excellence.

But the most practical information can be found in the Business Center at ftc.gov. There they outline "advertising and marketing basics" that every social media professional should be familiar with. The list includes:

Advertising and Marketing Basics

Under the law, claims in advertisements must be truthful, cannot be deceptive or unfair, and must be evidence-based. For some specialized products or services, additional rules may apply.

Children

If you advertise directly to children or market kid-related products to their parents, it's important to comply with truth-in-advertising standards. (Questions about kids' privacy? Check out the FTC's resources about COPPA, the Children's

Online Privacy Protection Act. The FTC also has a special page about food advertising to children and adolescents.)

Endorsements

Do you use endorsements in your marketing? Do they meet the standards of the FTC Act and the FTC's Guides Concerning Use of Endorsements and Testimonials in Advertising (Endorsement Guides)? Find out more by consulting FTC compliance resources.

Testimonial
A statement verifying the quality or character of a product or individual.

Environmental Marketing

Companies are offering consumers an ever-growing assortment of "green" options. But whether your environmental claims are about the product or the packaging, you'll need competent and reliable scientific evidence to support what you say. Find out more by consulting the FTC's revised Green Guides. Have you spotted what you think might be a deceptive claim or practice? File a complaint.

Health Claims

Companies must support their advertising claims with solid proof. This is especially true for businesses that market food, over-the-counter drugs, dietary supplements, contact lenses, and other health-related products.

Made in USA

Do you promote your products as "Made in the USA"? Under the law, some products must disclose U.S. content. For others, manufacturers and marketers who choose to make claims about the amount of U.S. content need to know about the FTC's Enforcement Policy Statement on U.S. Origin Claims. Is your company up on what's required?

Online Advertising and Marketing

The internet connects marketers to customers across the country and around the world. If you advertise online, remember the rules and guidelines that protect consumers also help businesses by maintaining the credibility of the internet as a marketing medium. In addition, truth-in-advertising standards apply if you sell computers, software, apps, or other products or services.

Telemarketing

The FTC's Telemarketing Sales Rule helps protect consumers from fraudulent telemarketing calls and gives them certain protections under the National Do Not Call Registry. Companies also need to be familiar with rules banning most forms of robocalling. If you or someone working on your behalf is telemarketing products or services, know the dos and don'ts before you plan your strategy.

More About Endorsements

Each of the previous categories is relevant to different organizations to varying degrees, but almost every business uses endorsements to one extent or another. The FTC website has a detailed guide written in plain English that answers some of the most commonly asked questions about endorsements. The following are some of the excerpts most relevant to social media work, but it is a good idea for any marketing professional to read the entire list and check back frequently for updates.

Do the Endorsement Guides apply to social media?

Yes. Truth in advertising is important in all media, whether they have been around for decades (like television and magazines) or are relatively new (like blogs and social media).

Isn't it common knowledge that bloggers are paid to tout products or that if you click a link on a blogger's site to buy a product, the blogger will get a commission?

No. Some bloggers who mention products in their posts have no connection to the marketers of those products – they don't receive anything for their reviews or get a commission. They simply recommend those products to their readers because they believe in them. Moreover, the financial arrangements between

> **Deceptive Endorsement**
>
> A public statement of approval that is somehow misleading. For example, a video of an actor wearing a white lab coat recommending a vitamin supplement would be deceptive because people would assume she was a physician.

some bloggers and advertisers may be apparent to industry insiders, but not to everyone else who reads a particular blog. Under the law, an act or practice is deceptive if it misleads "a significant minority" of consumers. Even if some readers are aware of these deals, many readers aren't. That's why disclosure is important.

Are you monitoring bloggers?

Generally not, but if concerns about possible violations of the FTC Act come to our attention, we'll evaluate them case by case. If law enforcement becomes necessary, our focus usually will be on advertisers or their ad agencies and public relations firms. Action against an individual endorser, however, might be appropriate in certain circumstances.

Does the FTC hold online reviewers to a higher standard than reviewers for paper-and-ink publications?

No. The FTC Act applies across the board. The issue is – and always has been – whether the audience understands the reviewer's relationship to the company whose products are being recommended. If the audience understands the relationship, a disclosure isn't needed.

If you're employed by a newspaper or TV station to give reviews – whether online or offline – your audience probably understands that your job is to provide your personal opinion on behalf of the newspaper or television station. In that situation, it's clear that you did not buy the product yourself – whether it's a book or a car or a movie ticket. On a personal blog, a social networking page, or in similar media, the reader might not realize that the reviewer has a relationship with the company whose products are being recommended. Disclosure of that relationship helps readers decide how much weight to give the review.

I'm a blogger. I heard that every time I mention a product on my blog, I have to say whether I got it for free or paid for it myself. Is that true?

No. If you mention a product you paid for yourself, there isn't an issue. Nor is it an issue if you get the product for free because a store is giving out free samples to its customers.

The FTC is only concerned about endorsements that are made on behalf of a sponsoring advertiser. For example, an endorsement would be covered by the FTC Act if an advertiser – or someone working for an advertiser – pays you or gives you something of value to mention a product. If you receive free products or other perks with the expectation that you'll promote or discuss the advertiser's products in your blog, you're covered. Bloggers who are part of network marketing programs where they sign up to receive free product samples in exchange for writing about them also are covered.

What if all I get from a company is a $1-off coupon, an entry in a sweepstakes or a contest, or a product that is only worth a few dollars? Does that still have to be disclosed?

The question you need to ask is whether knowing about that gift or incentive would affect the weight or credibility your readers give to your recommendation. If it could, then it should be disclosed. For example, being entered into a sweepstakes or a contest for a chance to win a thousand dollars in exchange for an endorsement could very well affect how people view that endorsement. Determining whether a small gift would affect the weight or credibility of an endorsement could be difficult. It's always safer to disclose that information.

Also, even if getting one free item that's not very valuable doesn't affect your credibility, continually getting free stuff from an advertiser or multiple advertisers could suggest you expect future benefits from positive reviews. If a blogger or other endorser has a relationship with a marketer or a network that sends freebies in the hope of positive reviews, it's best to let readers know about the free stuff.

Even an incentive with no financial value might affect the credibility of an endorsement and would need to be disclosed. The Guides give the example of a restaurant patron being offered the opportunity to appear in television advertising before giving his opinion about a product. Because the chance to appear in a TV ad could sway what someone says, that incentive should be disclosed.

What if I upload a video to YouTube that shows me reviewing several products? Should I disclose when I got them from an advertiser?

Yes. The guidance for videos is the same as for websites or blogs.

What if I return the product after I review it? Should I still make a disclosure?

That might depend on the product and how long you are allowed to use it. For example, if you get free use of a car for a month, we recommend a disclosure even though you have to return it. But even for less valuable products, it's best to be open and transparent with your readers.

I have a website that reviews local restaurants. It's clear when a restaurant pays for an ad on my website, but do I have to disclose which restaurants give me free meals?

If you get free meals, you should let your readers know so they can factor that in when they read your reviews. Some readers might conclude that if a restaurant gave you a free meal because it knew you were going to write a review, you might have gotten special food or service.

A trade association hired me to be its "ambassador" and promote its upcoming conference in social media, primarily on Facebook, Twitter, and in my blog. The association is only hiring me for five hours a week. I disclose my relationship with the association in my blogs and in the tweets and posts I make about the event during the hours I'm working. But sometimes I get questions about the conference in my off time. If I respond via Twitter when I'm not officially working, do I need to make a disclosure? Can that be solved by placing a badge for the conference in my Twitter profile?

You have a financial connection to the company that hired you and that relationship exists whether or not you are being paid for a particular tweet. If you are endorsing the conference in your tweets, your audience has a right to know about your relationship. That said, some of your tweets responding to questions about the event might not be endorsements, because they aren't communicating your opinions about the conference (for example, if someone just asks you for a link to the conference agenda).

Also, if you respond to someone's questions about the event via email or text, that person probably already knows your affiliation or they wouldn't be asking you. You probably wouldn't need a disclosure in that context. But when you respond via social media, all your followers see your posts and some of them might not have seen your earlier disclosures.

With respect to posting the conference's badge on your Twitter profile page, a disclosure on a profile page isn't sufficient because many people in your audience probably won't see it. Also, depending upon what it says, the badge may not adequately inform consumers of your connection to the trade association. If it's simply a logo or hashtag for the event, it won't tell consumers of your relationship to the association.

I share in my social media posts about products I use. Do I actually have to say something positive about a product for my posts to be endorsements covered by the FTC Act?

Simply posting a picture of a product in social media, such as on Pinterest, or a video of you using it could convey that you like and approve of the product. If it does, it's an endorsement.

You don't necessarily have to use words to convey a positive message. If your audience thinks that what you say or otherwise communicate about a product reflects your opinions or beliefs about the product, and you have a relationship with the company marketing the product, it's an endorsement subject to the FTC Act.

Of course, if you don't have any relationship with the advertiser, then your posts simply are not subject to the FTC Act, no matter what you show or say about the product. The FTC Act covers only endorsements made on behalf of a sponsoring advertiser.

My Facebook page identifies my employer. Should I include an additional disclosure when I post on Facebook about how useful one of our products is?

It's a good idea. People reading your posts in their news feed – or on your profile page – might not know where you work or what products your employer makes. Many businesses are so diversified that readers might not realize that the products you're talking about are sold by your company.

Is there special wording I have to use to make the disclosure?

No. The point is to give readers the essential information. A simple disclosure like "Company X gave me this product to try . . . ." will usually be effective.

Do I have to hire a lawyer to help me write a disclosure?

No. What matters is effective communication, not legalese. A disclosure like "Company X sent me [name of product] to try, and I think it's great" gives your readers the information they need. Or, at the start of a short video, you might say, "Some of the products I'm going to use in this video were sent to me by their manufacturers." That gives the necessary heads-up to your viewers.

When should I say more than that I got a product for free?

It depends on what else (if anything) you received from the company.

For example, if an app developer gave you their 99-cent app for free in order for you to review it, that might not have much effect on the weight that readers give to your review. But if the app developer also gave you $100, that would have a much greater effect on the credibility of your review. So a disclosure that simply said you got the app for free wouldn't be good enough.

Similarly, if a company gave you a $50 gift card to give away to one of your readers and a second $50 gift card to keep for yourself, it wouldn't be good enough to only say that the company gave you a gift card to give away.

As you can see by the various considerations the FTC looks at in many of the above examples, there are very few clear-cut answers when it comes to endorsements. If you're adding endorsements – or even one new kind of endorsement or approach – check with a legal professional to make sure you're following all of the applicable rules.

Despite the many different considerations advertisers might have to consider, there are themes associated with the FTC's decision-making process. When organizing endorsements, to increase the chances of a successful and legal approach, ask yourself the following question: Is there any way a consumer could be misled by the endorsement(s) we are seeking?

It's also important to remember that, though it may seem intimidating, the list of guidelines provided by the FTC to protect the consumer protects the business owner, too. After all, you might be tempted to share an endorsement that's misleading as a way of gaining short-term positive results. That decision is likely to hurt your brand in the long run. The FTC guidelines can help business owners make good decisions.

The previous list includes some of the information social media professionals should consider regarding endorsements, but there is additional information regarding product placement, celebrity endorsements, and soliciting endorsements that is important as well. Even if the approach doesn't immediately and directly apply to your organization, it's important to have a basic understanding of what's on the list.

What does the FTC say about social media contests?

Surprisingly, as of December 2016, the FTC doesn't have a lot of information on their website about social media contests specifically, but they do address contests that generate content that could be considered an endorsement.

My company runs contests and sweepstakes in social media. To enter, participants have to send a Tweet or make a pin with the hashtag, #XYZ_Rocks. ("XYZ" is the name of my product.) Isn't that enough to notify readers that the posts were incentivized?

No. It's likely that many readers would not understand such a hashtag to mean that those posts were made as part of a contest or that the people doing the posting had received something of value (in this case, a chance to win the contest prize). Making the word "contest" or "sweepstakes" part of the hashtag should be enough. However, the word "sweeps" probably isn't, because it is likely that many people would not understand what that means.

One important consideration for any social media professional to remember is that *each platform* is likely to have its own guideline for contests – as well as the general guidelines you need to consider. It's common to run contests on multiple platforms, so if that's your approach, remember to check the guidelines for each platform separately.

What is COPPA?

According to the FTC website:

Congress enacted the Children's Online Privacy Protection Act (COPPA) in 1998. COPPA required the Federal Trade Commission to issue and enforce regulations concerning children's online privacy. The Commission's original COPPA Rule became effective on April 21, 2000. The Commission issued an amended Rule on December 19, 2012. The amended Rule took effect on July 1, 2013.

The primary goal of COPPA is to place parents in control over what information is collected from their young children online. The Rule was designed to protect children under age 13 while accounting for the dynamic nature of the Internet. The Rule applies to operators of commercial websites and online services (including mobile apps) directed to children under 13 that collect, use, or disclose personal information from children, and operators of general audience websites or online services with actual knowledge that they are collecting, using, or disclosing personal information from children under 13. The Rule also applies to websites or online services that have actual knowledge that they are collecting personal information directly from users of another website or online service directed to children.

If you are covered by COPPA, you must do the following:

1. Post a clear and comprehensive online privacy policy describing their information practices for personal information collected online from children;
2. Provide direct notice to parents and obtain verifiable parental consent, with limited exceptions, before collecting personal information online from children;
3. Give parents the choice of consenting to the operator's collection and internal use of a child's information, but prohibiting the operator from disclosing that information to third parties (unless disclosure is integral to the site or service, in which case, this must be made clear to parents);
4. Provide parents access to their child's personal information to review and/or have the information deleted;
5. Give parents the opportunity to prevent further use or online collection of a child's personal information;
6. Maintain the confidentiality, security, and integrity of information they collect from children, including by taking reasonable steps to release such information only to parties capable of maintaining its confidentiality and security; and
7. Retain personal information collected online from a child for only as long as is necessary to fulfill the purpose for which it was collected and delete the information using reasonable measures to protect against its unauthorized access or use.

The FTC is also very clear in defining what "personal information" includes under COPPA guidelines.

- First and last name;
- A home or other physical address including street name and name of a city or town;
- Online contact information;

- A screen or user name that functions as online contact information;
- A telephone number;
- A social security number;
- A persistent identifier that can be used to recognize a user over time and across different websites or online services;
- A photograph, video, or audio file, where such file contains a child's image or voice;
- Geolocation information sufficient to identify street name and name of a city or town; or
- Information concerning the child or the parents of that child that the operator collects online from the child and combines with an identifier described above.

If you're not sure if COPPA is something that pertains to your business, consult your legal advisor. It's important to remember that many brands may not seem like they fall under COPPA, but through growth and the addition of new lines, product offerings could change enough to make the guidelines relevant to your business. It should be an ongoing consideration of a social media strategist even if it isn't applicable to your organization today.

What happens if you do violate an FTC regulation?

It is well worth your time to review the FTC guidelines and, in general, avoid ethically questionable practices. The cost of a violation will vary greatly depending on the infraction, of course, but you have to consider more than just the possibility of a fine. You'll likely need to hire legal support and you'll definitely spend a good amount of your valuable time working on your response – not to mention the potential damage to your reputation. There are so many variables, it's impossible to estimate the cost of an infraction, but the good news is that violations are avoidable with continuing education, the right legal support, and consistently ethical decisions.

Chapter 5 Discussion

1. Visit the FTC website and review the entire list of Frequently Asked Questions. (Only a portion of the questions is shared in this book.) Note any additional FAQs that you found relevant.

2. Review the FTC website in detail and answer the following questions:

   a. How would you explain the role of the FTC to someone who had never heard of the organization before?

   b. What information (perhaps outside of social media) was new to you?

   c. What three pieces of information do you think are critical to share with your clients, team, leaders, or key stakeholders? When deciding, consider what might be most relevant to them, what could lead to the most costly mistakes, and what they are least likely to know or understand.

Part Three
Social Media Policy

Chapter 6

Creating Your Social Media Policy

Though social media has become more recognized as a valid – even required – component of any marketing plan, you may still find yourself in a situation where you need to update or even create a social media policy for an organization. Deciding what it should include isn't a job for one person – but you might be the one person who needs to begin the process and guide the subject matter experts.

A social media professional's goals for a social media strategy are simple:

- Create a social media policy to govern the activities of everyone associated with the organization. This policy will be used to educate, so it should be written in clear language. But it will also be used for compliance, so it should be reviewed and approved by your organization's legal counsel.
- Support everyone in the organization – peers, leaders, consultants, key stakeholders – as they read and attempt to understand how the social media policy applies to them in their personal and professional engagements. Recommend that social media training be included in new employee orientations and that regular trainings be provided for all employees to help everyone keep up with the changes in the industry.
- Update the policy as needed to reflect the current market, organizational changes, and changes in social media.

While understanding the purpose of a social media strategy creation at a high level may be easily broken into three key considerations, filling in the details is a little more challenging. Every industry and organization has unique considerations and, because social media law is still evolving, legal experts may not always agree on what a company should and shouldn't do. With that in mind, we've gathered information to help guide you in the process of crafting your social media policy or reading and updating the policy you currently have in place. Ideally, this will guide your research, so you can provide informed suggestions for your organization to consider.

What should you consider including in your social media policy?

Who

Clearly outline who responds to customers. In some instances, this may be simple – there may be one person who responds to everything. In other cases, you may have a team who responds and certain individuals may have areas of expertise, so specific questions and comments may be reserved for them. Another common response is – if this is a common concern for your industry or organization – to send certain comments straight to a legal professional for guidance.

Identify who the policy applies to. Especially if you have a variety of employee job types (full-time, part-time, contract, etc.), specify who is expected to abide by the policy.

Disclose any relationships or affiliations. Don't assume everyone in your organization understands each of your brands, the markets they're in, and any partnerships that may be associated with that reach.

What

Clearly state what information cannot be shared. Never assume employees understand what information is confidential or proprietary. Be as specific as possible, but also include broad terms as appropriate. For example, you might provide an example (specific) followed by a detailed description of why the information could not be shared. This is an area in which individual leaders within the organization can be helpful by providing feedback and guidance to individual employees.

Establish clear guideline for using company logos, trademarks, etc. Typically, organizations will simply ask that employees not use company images, but during fundraisers or promotions, you may want to provide different recommendations.

> **Do you need a Defamation Response Process and Policy?** This policy is the systematic approach members of an organization take in response to an act of defamation. Each organization has a different defamation risk level and should take that into consideration when creating the policy and what details and examples would be most helpful.

Where

Clarify what platforms the policy applies to. If you currently or someday might have social networking sites, websites, internal and external sharing sites, blogs, wikis, etc., include them in a list to ensure each employee understands the depth and breadth of the policy.

When

Establish clear and reasonable response times. Once you have established who is responding, set expectations for how quickly consumers should receive a reply. If your organization has a strong national or international customer base, it's important to consider how to manage activity around the clock.

A few specific questions you might consider answering include:

1. When is the employee expected to respond (work hours only, special response times during promotions,

etc.)? Consider employment laws carefully when setting these expectations. In some circumstances, those guidelines will dictate what you can and can't have an employee do.

2. If there are multiple employees available, what shift does everyone take to ensure coverage and avoid multiple people responding to the same question?

3. Do different kinds of concerns warrant different response times? You might have a one-hour maximum response time for a concern posted but a three-hour maximum for general questions. For ease of implementation, keep the guidelines as simple as possible and only introduce alternative requirements if necessary.

Why

For each request, explain why adherence is important. Employees are more likely to accept and remember the details of a policy if you explain why the guideline exists. And if you can't explain why, it's a good indication you might want to reconsider the policy in general.

How

Establish best practices for commenting and responding publicly. Do you want employees to respond to customers online? If a consumer is upset, does every employee know how to transition them from a public platform to a private conversation? It's important to clarify as many potential scenarios as you can so the employee is prepared for them when they arise.

If an employee comments on any aspect of the company's business, require that they identify themselves as such and include a disclaimer that they are responding as an individual, not on behalf of the organization. In the NISM book *Online Community Management: Grow and Develop an Active Audience on Social Media*, you'll find additional information about how to respond to feedback online – particularly challenging or negative feedback.

Help everyone anticipate and manage any potential ethical challenges. If you aren't concerned about ethical dilemmas that may arise on social media, you might simply add a reminder to respond professionally or share the organization's values. There are definitely some companies with less risk than others. (Consider a jewelry store compared to a religious organization.) However, if you are able to anticipate ethical challenges or risky situations – even if it is possible they may never happen – consider outlining specifically how situations are to be managed. The guidelines can be as simple as, "Do nothing online and notify your supervisor immediately" to step-by-step guidance for the employees can respond to the situation themselves.

It's important that the guidance you provide in your social media policy is supportive of activity. Be careful not to leave people fearful of making a mistake or so confused they don't even know where to start.

If you're creating your social media strategy from scratch, in addition to reviewing the format of other documents used successfully within your organization, it might also be helpful to look at policies other organizations – ideally ones similar to yours – have posted online. We've included several examples of social media policies in the additional materials of this book, but you can also search the internet for organizations that publicly share their resources.

Within your social media policy and in addition to any discussion of intellectual property, you might consider including the following specific policies that will answer some of the questions listed above.

> A *Corporate Privacy Policy* outlines how an organization gathers, manages, and discloses some or all of its customer and client information. It is sometimes simply called a privacy policy.

A *Proper Use Policy*, made up of a set of rules created by the owner or administrator of a website or service, details the ways in which content may be used. This kind of policy is sometimes called a *Responsible Use Policy*.

A *Dispute Resolution Process* can be used to resolve an issue between parties and is helpful to have in place *before* an issue arises so the situation can be addressed quickly. Being prepared with a systematic approach for dispute resolution also helps people see that your approach is fair. Common approaches to dispute resolution include litigation, negotiation, mediation, and arbitration.

Updating Your Social Media Policy

Once you've created your social media policy, it's important to set up a regular review schedule to ensure it is updated as needed – at minimum once a year, but more often if your organization reviews other policies or plans within the organization on a more frequent basis. Reasons you might need to update your social media strategy include, but are not limited to:

- Changes in your industry (tightened or relaxed regulations, a new competitor, etc.)
- Changes in your organization (a new customer market, product line, etc.)
- The integration of a new market – especially if there are international considerations
- New social media platforms (either new to everyone or just new to your organization)
- Lessons learned (if a situation came up that wasn't accounted for in the policy, you might have handled it in the moment and added a description to policy for future use)

- Opportunities you've uncovered to work between departments – either to share complementing information or avoid sharing conflicting content

The following is a memo that was shared publicly by the *Los Angeles Times* when they updated their social media policy. They posted this on their website so their employees and their current and potential customers could be made aware of the changes. Examples like this provide the opportunity for us to consider what the best approach would be for our organizations.

Memo from the Los Angeles Times Standards and Practices Committee

Colleagues,

As you know, the Standards and Practices Committee issued newsroom guidelines in March on using social media. We have now revised and organized them in a way we believe is easier to use (see below).

Although the document addresses a few new situations that have arisen in the last several months, the underlying principle is unchanged, one best expressed in the opening passage of our Ethics Guidelines: The Times is to be, above all else, a principled news organization. In deed and in appearance, journalists must keep themselves – and The Times – above reproach.

Your professional life and your personal life are intertwined in the online world, just as they are offline. Attempts, for instance, to distinguish your high school friends from your professional associates are fine, but in all spaces one should adhere to the principle that as an editorial employee you are responsible for maintaining The Times' credibility.

As in March, we note that the guidelines apply to all editorial employees, whether you work in print or on the Web, or you are a reporter, editor, photographer, blogger, producer, designer, artist – whatever your job. Even if you aren't using social media tools yet, you might want to someday, so please familiarize yourself with the standards.

This document is part of a series of guidelines crafted to help all of us navigate the continually changing world of covering the news. The methods and mediums may change, but our standards do not. These guidelines and those about moderating reader comments, using photos online, handling corrections and dealing with obscenity issues can always be found on The Times' library's intranet site.

There you also will find the complete Los Angeles Times Ethics Guidelines, the statement of principles and standards from which all others follow.

– Russ Stanton
Henry Fuhrmann
on behalf of the Standards and Practices Committee

The *LA Times* capitalized on the opportunity to update their social media policy by reminding all of the readers – customers, potential customers and employees – of the organization's ethics and existing policies. Their careful wording serves as an excellent example of how we can use social media policy creation and updates to educate users and boost our own reputation.

Chapter 6 Discussion

1. Locate your organization's social media policy. (If they don't have one, find a company that has theirs posted online.) Review each of the bold words and phrases in this chapter and see if they are represented in the policy you're reading.

   a. If they are, are they clear and concise?

   b. If they aren't, can you think of a reason why they wouldn't be relevant?

3. Find three social media professionals working in three different organizations. Ask them the following questions and compare their answers, considering why their responses may have varied.

   a. Do you know how to access the social media policy for your organization?

   ii. If no, ask if they would be willing to try and to let you know what they find.

   iii. If yes, ask them if they can remember what content it contains and how it is used.

Part Four
The SMS Exam

Chapter 7

What do you need to know for the SMS exam?

The NISM textbooks are designed to help you prepare for the SMS exam *and more*. Our goal is to support social media professionals preparing to take the certified SMS exam to pass the test, but we also want to leave every reader with a detailed view of what the social media landscape looks like today and how they can effectively navigate it. But what if completing your certification is your top priority? Here's where we recommend you focus.

Monitor terms of service to protect company's intellectual property interests.

This book began by discussing a really important question: What is your organization's intellectual property? There are many options – and many legal terms to consider that might help you identify all of the content you should be protecting.

In the first section and throughout the book, there are many legal terms (copyright, trademark, parody, etc.) that can help you understand how to protect your organization and avoid infringing on the rights of others. Though to a certain extent it's impossible to avoid simply memorizing the definitions of these terms, our goal was to organize them throughout the book in a way that would make them easier to understand and remember. Many of these terms tie back to intellectual property and creative works, so we recommend you begin by exploring what that includes for your organization and then integrate the additional language as you move through the rest of the book.

Understand how to create a social media policy to govern activities within an organization.

We provided you with a list of considerations for creating a social media policy – who, what, where, when, why, and how. It's important to review that list and understand how to address each of the points included. In this case – like many others – we recommend an experiential approach to exploring these topics. Look at your organization's social media policy (create one if needed) and apply everything you've read, exploring additional resources as needed. This real-world application will help you retain the information.

There are also several sample social media policies available in the additional resources section of this book and countless others available online. You might find reviewing how other organizations designed their policies helpful, but it's important to review the information with a critical eye. Just because someone wrote a social media policy doesn't mean they wrote it *correctly*. Look at their content and approach, compare it to what you have learned, and decide what you would do the same and what you would do differently. You will find that no two policies are exactly the same and that it's okay. You need to make sure that your social media policy fits your organization's persona and goals, and helps to support the culture your employees create and thrive in. This means that some policies will be extremely relaxed and laid back, while others may be very heavy in legal language.

Create a procedure explaining how to (and when *not* to) participate on social media.

One specific component that's important to call out in your social media policy is clear direction for employees regarding when and how to engage on public and private platforms.

This will vary greatly by organization, but it's critical for every social media policy. Without specific direction, your employees are likely to make one of two mistakes: they'll engage in a way that doesn't align with the organization's desired approach or they won't engage at all.

In some cases, you may not want employees to be active on social media. For example, if you work in a highly regulated industry, the risk may be too great. If there is less risk in your industry, you may want employees to respond quickly and have fun with your customers. For example, if you were managing the social media platform associated with a sports team, multiple employees chiming in and rooting along with the fans would be a great way to keep the energy up.

There isn't a single right answer. But as a social media professional, it's your job to make sure you're continually asking the right questions and providing ideas and support for others.

Maintain social media policy as change occurs.

Part of your role as a social media strategist is to update the organization's social media policy. This is an ongoing process that needs frequent attention but is a manageable process if approached often and systematically. We recommend a quick review of your policy on a quarterly basis and an in-depth review annually, but depending on your industry, developments in your organization, how robust the policy is to begin with, etc. you may want to review the material more frequently.

When approaching your review, consider at minimum the following possible reasons for updating details within your policy:

- Changes in your industry
- Changes in your organization
- New social media platforms
- Lessons learned (likely a positive or negative high-profile experience)

Work with key stakeholders to ensure efforts are supported.

As always, it's a critical responsibility of a social media professional to keep key stakeholders in the loop. Depending on the design of your organization, this may include your legal department, team members, advisors, leaders, investors, or your marketing department. And depending on where you are in the process of developing your social media policy, this may include high-level or detailed updates. Whatever is right for your organization, it's important to set up routine communication that key stakeholders will read or listen to and understand. This will keep them from withdrawing their support down the road at a critical time and will allow you to move forward with ease.

Additional Resources

Sample Social Media Policies

The following are social media policies that – each in their own way – are well-constructed and designed to support employee education and compliance. Consider how each of them may have components that will work well in your organization.

Intel

The Intel social media guidelines can be found here: http://www.intel.com/content/www/us/en/legal/intel-social-media-guidelines.html

Social media is changing the way we work, offering a new model to engage with customers, colleagues, and the world at large. We believe this kind of interaction can help you to build stronger, more successful business relationships. And it's a way for you to take part in global conversations related to the work we are doing at Intel and the things we care about.

These are the official guidelines for participating in social media for Intel. If you're an Intel employee or contractor creating or contributing to blogs, wikis, social networks, virtual worlds, or any other kind of social media, these guidelines are for you. They will evolve as new social networking tools emerge, so check back regularly to make sure you're up to date. If you are ever hesitant or unsure about something you are posting on your online resume or social channels, please contact Social.Media@intel.com

3 Rules of Engagement

Disclose
Your presence in social media must be transparent

Protect
Take extra care to protect both Intel and yourself

Use Common Sense
Remember that professional, straightforward and appropriate communication is best

1. Disclose

Your honesty—or dishonesty—will be quickly noticed in the social media environment. Please represent Intel ethically and with integrity.

Be transparent: If you make an endorsement or recommendation about Intel's products/technologies, you must disclose that you work for Intel. If you do not have an "Intel" handle, then use "#iwork4intel" in your postings. Using a disclaimer in your bio or profile is not enough per the FTC.

Be truthful: If you have a vested interest in something you are discussing, be the first to point it out and be specific about what it is.

Be yourself: Stick to your area of expertise; only write what you know. If you publish to a website outside Intel, please use a disclaimer like this one: "The postings on this site are my own and don't necessarily represent Intel's positions, strategies, or opinions."

Be up-to-date: If you are leaving Intel, please remember to update your employment information on social media sites.

2. Protect

Make sure all that transparency doesn't violate Intel's confidentiality or legal guidelines for commercial speech—or your own privacy. Remember, if you're online, you're on the record—everything on the Internet is public and searchable. And what you write is ultimately your responsibility.

Don't tell secrets: Never reveal Intel classified or confidential information. If you are posting your job description on LinkedIn, be sure not to reveal confidential product information. If you're unsure, check with Intel PR or Global Communications Group. Off-limit topics include litigation, non-published financials, and unreleased product info. Also, please respect brand, trademark, copyright, fair use, and trade secrets. If it gives you pause—pause rather than publish.

Don't slam the competition (or Intel): Play nice. Anything you publish must be true and not misleading, and all claims must be substantiated and approved.*

Don't overshare: Be careful out there—once you hit "share," you usually can't get it back. Plus, being judicious will help make your content more crisp and audience-relevant.

3. Use Common Sense

Perception is reality and in online social networks, the lines between public and private, personal and professional, are blurred. Just by identifying yourself as an Intel employee, you are creating perceptions about your expertise and about Intel. Do us all proud.

Add value: There are millions of words out there— make yours helpful and thought-provoking. Remember, it's a conversation, so keep it real. Build community by posting content that invites responses—then stay engaged. You can also broaden the dialogue by citing others who are writing about the same topic and allowing your content to be shared.

*Don't make claims: We must use FTC mandated disclaimers **in all communications** when benchmarking or comparing processors. So stay away from saying our products are smarter/ faster/higher-performing in your social media postings. Leave that to the experts.

Did you screw up? If you make a mistake, admit it. Be upfront and be quick with your correction. If you're posting to a blog, you may choose to modify an earlier post—just make it clear that you have done so.

Contractors and Endorsements

As the Intel Social Media Guidelines describes, we support transparency and are committed to clear disclosure of relationships and endorsements. If you are contracted, seeded, or in any way compensated by Intel to create social media, please be sure to read and follow the Intel Sponsored, Seeded, or Incentivized Social Media Practitioner Guidelines. As part of these guidelines, you need to disclose that you have been seeded or otherwise compensated by Intel. Your blog will be monitored for compliance with our guidelines and accurate descriptions of products and claims.

Moderation

Moderation (reviewing and approving content) applies to any social media content written on behalf of Intel by people outside the company, whether the site is on or off Intel.com. We do not endorse or take responsibility for content posted by third parties, also known as user-generated content (UGC). This includes text input and uploaded files, including video, images, audio, executables, and documents. While we strongly encourage user participation, there are some guidelines we ask third parties to follow to keep it safe for everyone.

Post moderation: Even when a site requires the user to register before posting, simple user name and email entry doesn't really validate the person. To ensure least risk/most security, we require moderation of all UGC posts. The designated moderator scans all posts to be sure they adhere to Intel's guidelines.

Community moderation (reactive moderation): For established, healthy communities, group moderation by regular users can work well. This will sometimes be allowed to take the place of post moderation—but it must be applied for and approved.

The "house rules": Whether content is post moderated or community moderated, we use this rule of thumb: the Good, the Bad, but not the Ugly. If the content is positive or negative and in context to the conversation, then it can be approved, regardless of whether it's favorable or unfavorable to Intel. But if the content is ugly, offensive, denigrating, and/or completely out of context, then we ask our moderators and communities to reject the content.

Intel Sponsored, Seeded, or Incentivized Social Media Practitioner Guidelines

Intel supports transparency. We are committed to ensuring that our social media practitioners (SMPs) clearly disclose relationships and endorsements, and that statements about Intel® products are truthful and substantiated. If you are a social media practitioner who has been seeded with product, incentivized, or otherwise has an ongoing relationship with Intel, these guidelines apply to you. If you have any questions or concerns about them, get in touch with your Intel sponsor.

Please keep in mind that Intel monitors social media related to our business, including the activities of our sponsored, seeded, or incentivized SMPs. If we find any non-disclosed relationships or statements that are false or misleading, we will contact you for correction. If, as a sponsored SMP, you are found to repetitively make inaccurate statements about Intel, Intel® products, or Intel® services, we may discontinue our relationship with you.

Rules of Engagement for Intel Sponsored, Seeded, or Incentivized SMPs

> **Be transparent:** Please clearly and conspicuously disclose your relationship to Intel, including any incentives or sponsorships. Be sure this information is readily apparent to the public and to readers of each of your posts.

> **Be specific:** Do not make general claims about Intel® products, but talk specifically about what you experienced.

> **Be yourself:** We encourage you to write in the first person and stick to your area of expertise as it relates to Intel® technology.

> **Be conscientious:** Keep in mind that what you write is your responsibility, and failure to abide by these guidelines could put your Intel sponsorship or incentive at risk. Also, please always follow the terms and conditions for any third-party sites in which you participate.

Los Angeles Times

SOCIAL MEDIA GUIDELINES

Social media networks – Facebook, MySpace, Twitter and others – provide useful reporting and promotional tools for Los Angeles Times journalists. The Times' Ethics Guidelines will largely cover issues that arise when using social media, but this brief document should provide additional guidance on specific questions.

Basic Principles

- Integrity is our most important commodity: Avoid writing or posting anything that would embarrass The Times or compromise your ability to do your job.
- Assume that your professional life and your personal life will merge online regardless of your care in separating them.
- Even if you use privacy tools (determining who can view your page or profile, for instance), assume that everything you write, exchange or receive on a social media site is public.
- Just as political bumper stickers and lawn signs are to be avoided in the offline world, so too are partisan expressions online.
- Be aware of perceptions. If you "friend" a source or join a group on one side of a debate, do so with the other side as well. Also understand that readers may view your participation in a group as your acceptance of its views; be clear that you're looking for story ideas or simply collecting information. Consider that you may be an observer of online content without actively participating.

Guidelines for Reporting

- Be aware of inadvertent disclosures or the perception of disclosures. For example, consider that "friending" a professional contact may publicly identify that person as one of your sources.
- You should identify yourself as a Times employee online if you would do so in a similar situation offline.
- Authentication is essential: Verify sourcing after collecting information online. When transmitting information online – as in re-Tweeting material from other sources – apply the same standards and level of caution you would in more formal publication.

Additional Notes

- Using social media sites means that you (and the content you exchange) are subject to their terms of service. This can have legal implications, including the possibility that your interactions could be subject to a third-party subpoena. The social media network has access to and control over everything you have disclosed to or on that site. For instance, any information might be turned over to law enforcement without your consent or even your knowledge.
- These passages from the "Outside affiliations and community work" section of the Ethics Guidelines may be helpful as you navigate social media sites. For the complete guidelines, please see The Times' library's intranet site or, if you are outside the company network, see the Readers' Representative Journal.

Editorial employees may not use their positions at the paper to promote personal agendas or causes. Nor should they allow their outside activities to undermine the impartiality of Times coverage, in fact or appearance.

Staff members may not engage in political advocacy – as members of a campaign or an organization specifically concerned with political change. Nor may they contribute money to a partisan campaign or candidate. No staff member may run for or accept appointment to any public office. Staff members should avoid public expressions or demonstrations of their political views – bumper stickers, lawn signs and the like.

Although The Times does not seek to restrict staff members' participation in civic life or journalistic organizations, they should be aware that outside affiliations and memberships may create real or apparent ethical conflicts. When those affiliations have even the slightest potential to damage the newspaper's credibility, staff members should proceed with caution and take care to advise supervisors.

Some types of civic participation may be deemed inappropriate. An environmental writer, for instance, would be prohibited from affiliating with environmental organizations, a health writer from joining medical groups, a business editor from membership in certain trade or financial associations.

– Standards and Practices Committee

Louisiana Tech University

http://www.latech.edu/administration/policies-and-procedures/1308.php

Policy 1308 - Online Social Media Usage Policy
Effective Date: 1/12/2015
Responsible Office: Office of the President

Overview

Louisiana Tech University unequivocally supports and endorses free speech and free expression amongst its students, faculty, and staff. While the University and its administration do not prohibit university personnel or student representatives from using social networking resources (including, but not limited to, Facebook, Twitter, Instagram, LinkedIn, Pinterest, blogs/vlogs, RSS feeds, podcasts, and postings to message boards), such usage should be done according to standards set forth by Louisiana Tech University for those who are communicating specifically and intentionally on behalf of or in an official capacity for the University. In addition to university standards, coaches and student-athletes must also adhere to all NCAA and athletic conference policies.

This Online Social Media Usage Policy and associated guidelines are designed to both educate university personnel and student representatives, and to enable the university to guide online social media communications used by persons who clearly identify themselves as an employee, representative, or student-athlete of Louisiana Tech University, and who intend to communicate specifically from that standpoint. The policy does not pertain to personal social media sites and accounts, or to those who are not communicating in an official capacity or on behalf of Louisiana Tech University.

Policy Objective

Louisiana Tech University's Online Social Media Usage Policy seeks to protect the image, reputation, integrity and mission of Louisiana Tech University through ensuring proper usage and identifying possible rule, policy and/or compliance issues.

Personnel Subject to Policy

The Online Social Media Usage Policy applies to:

Academic, administrative and/or research departments that establish a social media presence for the specific purpose of communicating on behalf of that entity and as a representative of the department or institution.

Student groups and organizations that are directly supported and overseen by, and registered with Louisiana Tech.

Student-athletes, SGA officers, student orientation leaders, and others identified as student representatives of Louisiana Tech, when acting or communicating as a representative of Louisiana Tech, either through a department or individually.

Any other personnel or representatives whose communications and/or actions via social media could result in penalties, fines, and/or sanctions against the university (i.e. student-athletes and NCAA and/or athletic conference rules violations, violations of non-disclosure agreements by faculty or staff, violations of FERPA or HIPAA confidentiality rules, etc.)

The Online Social Media Usage Policy does not apply to:

Individual students, faculty and/or staff who are communicating using their personal social media sites and accounts, or who are not communicating in an official capacity or on behalf of Louisiana Tech University.

Alumni and professional networks and/or organizations not officially sponsored by or associated with the university (unless using official Louisiana Tech logos or visual marks.)

Vendors and support organizations (unless using Louisiana Tech marks.)

Guidance and Compliance

All Louisiana Tech personnel and student representatives who clearly identify themselves as an employee, representative, student-athlete or student-leader of Louisiana Tech University, and who intend to communicate from that position and/or standpoint, should be aware that the institution reserves the right to monitor and guide all University-approved online social media sites that have been established for the expressed purpose of communication and providing information as official representatives of or source for the University.

Louisiana Tech personnel and student representatives, as described above, must acknowledge they have read, understand and agree to the university's Online Social Media Usage Policy, as published online.

Louisiana Tech personnel and student representatives, as described above, will be required to provide user names, aliases or other identities on social networking sites where they have clearly identified themselves as an employee, department or student representative of Louisiana Tech with the intent of communicating as an official representative of or source for the University.

Should the university discover materials or communications that are in violation of Louisiana Tech's Online Social Media Usage Policy, the employee/department or student representative, as described above, will be required to immediately remove the material.

Establishing and Maintaining a Social Media Account/Site (For University Faculty/Staff, Students and Departments)

Prior to establishing any social media accounts that are to be directly associated with or representative of Louisiana Tech, its departments, and/or programs, written permission from the department/unit head, dean or vice president, or other appropriate administrator, and from the Department of University Communications must be obtained. The site/account must have someone specifically assigned to updating and monitoring it regularly, as directed by the department/unit head. As it pertains to these official and approved social media sites:

Approved university, college or department logos must be used at all times.

Louisiana Tech social media sites must not be used for the endorsement of unrelated or personal products, causes, or political affiliations.

Do not post confidential information about Louisiana Tech students, employees, and other constituents. Employees must follow federal requirements such as FERPA, HIPAA, NCAA, and athletic conference regulations.

Do not use official university social media sites or personnel to interact, either by initiating or responding to a post or other communications, with prospective student-athletes (per NCAA rules and regulations.)

Do not use trademarked or copyrighted names, images, or content without written permission from the owner of the information/images or an authorized agent of the owner.

Do not place images of minors on any social media site or electronic communications medium without written and signed consent of the minor's parent or legal guardian.

Posting must follow University policy for conducting e-commerce and not disclose business transaction information such as credit card account numbers.

Posting by students on University social media sites must adhere to the University's code of conduct.

Postings may not be used to conduct political campaigning (excluding campus SGA elections.)

Louisiana Tech University reserves the right to demand immediate removal from University-affiliated social media accounts/sites materials which is abusive, defamatory, embarrassing, exploitative, harassing, hateful, illegal, injurious, libelous, obscene, pornographic, profane, threatening, or vulgar language or images, irrelevant or off-topic content, as well as spam or illicit advertising.

Glossary of Terms

Attribution
The act of identifying a person as the creator of a specific work.

Best Practices
A collection of expert advice based on individual and industry experience.

Black Hat
In a digital marketing campaign, this refers to techniques or practices that are illegal or unethical. They are usually completed by practitioners looking to get fast results, but those results rarely last as black hat practices are usually uncovered and the results reversed by search engines and platform owners. The opposite approach is called white hat.

Brand Equity
Commercial value associated with a product, based on consumer perception as opposed to the product or service itself.

Brandjacking
Securing the online identity of another individual or business for the purposes of acquiring that person's or business's brand equity.

Children's Online Privacy Protection Act of 1998 (COPPA)
An Act of Congress that governs the owners of organizations who target children under the age of 13.

Commercial Speech
Language used on behalf of an organization or individual to generate a profit.

Commercial Use
Any act or process that generates a profit.

Compliance
Obedience or conformity, typically in reference to an established law or policy.

Confidentiality
Pertaining to anything private that can't be disclosed to a wider group.

Consumer Privacy
Laws and regulations designed to protect individuals from loss of privacy due to failures of corporate customer privacy measures.

Contract
A written or spoken agreement between two or more parties meant to be enforceable by law.

Cookies
Messages from web servers shared to your browser when you visit internet sites.

Copyright
Legal right of ownership granted to the creator of any artistic work. In social media, this commonly refers to photography, art, video, and written work, but can cover any creative piece.

Copyright Violation
Any misuse of a protected artistic work.

Corporate Privacy Policy
How an organization gathers, manages, and discloses some or all of its customer and client information. Also called a privacy policy.

Creative Commons
A nonprofit organization that gathers cultural, educational, and scientific content in "the commons." The work in the commons is available to the public for free and legal sharing, use, repurposing, and remixing.

Cybersquatting
Registering internet domain names in the hope of reselling them at a profit.

Deceptive Endorsement
A public statement of approval that is somehow misleading. For example, a video of an actor wearing a white lab coat recommending a vitamin supplement would be deceptive because people would assume she was a physician.

Defamation
The act of damaging a person's reputation.

Defamation Response Process and Policy
The systematic response members of an organization take in response to an act of defamation.

Defamation Risk
The likelihood that you will be a target for defamation. Individuals and organizations have varying degrees of risk of defamation that may change over time.

Derivative Work
Work created from or based on existing work.

Dilution
Decreased value related to excessive use and/or increased availability.

Dispute Resolution
Process used to resolve an issue between parties. Common approaches include litigation, negotiation, mediation, and arbitration.

Endorsement
A public statement of approval.

Ethics
Moral principles that govern behavior.

Fair Use
Principle that supports the use of brief excerpts of copyright material under certain circumstances. Material may be quoted verbatim under fair use for criticism, news reporting, teaching, and research, without permission from or payment to the copyright holder.

Federal Trade Commission (FTC)
An independent agency of the United States government that promotes consumer protection and concerns itself with the prevention of anticompetitive business practices, such as coercive monopoly.

Governance
Directing a group through structured, sustained, and regulated processes to abide by laws and norms.

Infringement
Use without permission of an invention for which someone else owns a patent, copyright or trademark, whether the violation was intentional or not.

Intellectual Property

Work that is the result of creativity to which one has rights and for which one may apply for a patent, copyright, or trademark.

Lampooning

Satire or ridicule directed at an individual, institution, or item, focused on the character or behavior of the same.

License

Permission from an approved figure to own or use something, or perform a trade.

Non-commercial Use

Actions not primarily intended for compensation.

Parody

An exaggerated comedic imitation of the style of a particular individual or group.

Patent

Government license awarding a right for a set period that prohibits others from making, selling, or using the item described. In social media, patents are often sought for apps, processes, and tools.

Privacy

The right of an individual or group to selectively withdraw information about themselves.

Privacy Policy

How an organization gathers, manages, and discloses some or all of its customer and client information. Also called a Corporate Privacy Policy.

Proper Use Policy
Set of rules created by the owner or administrator of a website or service, that details the ways in which content may be used. Also called a Responsible Use Policy.

Proprietary Information
Processes, items and methods used in business which an organization wishes to keep private. Proprietary information is often associated with a competitive edge. Also called trade secrets.

Publicity Rights
Control of the commercial use of a name, image, likeness, or other aspects of an identity.

Registered Copyright
Date and content of a protected work recorded through a verifiable government source.

Registered Trademark
Word or symbol registered with a national trademark office.

Responsible Use Policy
Set of rules created by the owner or administrator of a website or service that details the ways in which content may be used. Also called a Proper Use Policy.

Safe Harbor Laws
Certain conduct deemed not to violate a specific rule, typically as the result of a connection with a separate and less specific rule.

Share Alike Use
Copyright licensing term that requires copies or adaptations of a work be released under the same or similar license as the original.

Terms of Service
Rules and guidelines created by an organization that a user must agree to in order to use your product or service.

Testimonial
A statement verifying the quality or character of a product or individual.

Trademark
Symbol, word, or words legally registered or established by use as representing a company or product.

Trade Secrets
Processes, items and methods used in business which an organization wishes to keep private. Trade secrets are often associated with a competitive edge. Also called proprietary information.

Waiver
Statement giving up a right.

White Hat
In a digital marketing campaign, this refers to techniques or practices that are legal and ethical. The opposite approach is called black hat.